In the
Silence

In the *Silence*

MEDITATIONS *for* EUCHARISTIC ADORATION

Vandy Brennan Nies

Liguori

ONE LIGUORI DRIVE
LIGUORI MO 63057-9999

Imprimi Potest:
Thomas D. Picton, C.Ss.R.
Provincial, Denver Province
The Redemptorists

Published by Liguori Publications
Liguori, Missouri
To order, call 800-325-9521
www.liguori.org

Library of Congress Cataloging-in-Publication Data
Nies, Vandy Brennan.
   In the silence : meditations for Eucharistic adoration / Vandy Brennan Nies.—
1st ed.
      p. cm.
   ISBN 978-0-7648-1886-8
   1. Lord's Supper—Adoration. 2. Lord's Supper—Meditations. 3. Lord's Supper—
Catholic Church. I. Title.
   BX2233.N54 2010
   264'.02036—dc22

                                                                    2009041374

Liguori Publications, a nonprofit corporation, is an apostolate of the Redemptorists.
To learn more about the Redemptorists, visit Redemptorists.com.

Printed in the United States of America
18 17 16 15 14 / 7 6 5 4 3
First edition

To my heavenly Mother, Queen of the Cenacle, whose entire life was an invitation to "Adore My Son"; and to my earthly parents, Virginia and Andrew Brennan, who taught me how to accept the invitation.

Then they told what had happened on the road,
and how he had been made known to them
in the breaking of the bread.

LUKE 24:35

Acknowledgments

My prayerful gratitude to:

» Those who touched my heart with their faith—parents and grandparents in particular, dedicated teachers, sisters and priests—whose belief in and reverence for Jesus in the Eucharist instilled in me a love for the Mass and eucharistic adoration;

» The members of my family—all four generations of them—whose support for my insatiable bent for writing has been constant, even when it required sacrifice on their part;

» The people whose insistent persuasion was a motivation to write this book as an instrument of spreading love for the Eucharist;

» My friend and spiritual companion, Fr. Ralph Wright, OSB, for his spiritual and journalistic advice;

» My writer/editor son, Jay Nies, whose filial support and professional insight and encouragement have been invaluable.

Contents

Foreword

In the *Imitation of Christ,* Thomas à Kempis wrote:

"Then God himself will say to me: 'If you want to be with me, I want to be with you.' And I will reply to him, 'Be generous enough to stay with me, Lord, it would please me and I would very much like to be with you. This is the whole of my desire that my heart should be united with yours.'"

Vandy Brennan Nies's meditations on the Eucharist are a wonderful, down to earth, invigorating, and prayerful example of this "desire." In an unobtrusive and refreshing way, while meditating on texts from Scripture, she leads us along her pathway of prayer and a nonchalant intimacy with the Lord. As she brings all of herself to these "Emmanuel moments" of adoration, I found, depending on my mood, that I was able to identify with her frustrations, her wonder, her desolation, and her thanksgiving.

Here is a book that will draw many people to a deeper love of Jesus, present in the Eucharist, and a deeper appreciation of our ongoing union with him. Out of her silence, she offers in words fresh ways to "abide" with the Lord.

RALPH WRIGHT, OSB
ST. LOUIS ABBEY

Introduction

The Will and Testament of Jesus

When Jesus uttered the words, "This is my body given up for you," on the night before he died, in effect he was writing his last will and testament. This God-man had accrued no wealth and no possessions; he had no earthly belongings to entrust to us. But when he returned to the Father, he certainly didn't leave us empty-handed. He left for us our greatest treasure.

In the absence of worldly belongings, he bequeathed himself to us for always and ever. He had reached the point where his mission was about to be fulfilled. He could return to the Father free of human constraints, having done what he was sent to do. Instead, he chose to initiate a plan to remain with us until the end of time in the tabernacles and monstrances of our churches—and in the hearts and souls of those he called his.

Setting the Tone for Eucharistic Adoration

As Catholics, we believe Jesus is present here—both human and divine—true God and true man. Because our faith tells us Jesus remains with us in the consecrated host and that he is the Real Presence on this altar, we come to spend time and adore him from the depths of our hearts. Adoration is a time for us to share with Jesus in the most intimate exchange.

Go to the Lord just as you are. Be natural. Turn yourself over to Jesus totally. Drain yourself of everything else that was important to you, regardless of how monumental or how mundane, until you walked into this church.

Now, nothing else matters. He has been waiting patiently for you to choose this time with him. Give it freely and fully! Allow him into the deepest recesses of your heart, even the places that are difficult for you to let him see.

You are invited to fall deeper in love with the Most Holy Sacrament—to leave here totally immersed in who he is—with a resolve to share him with each person you meet as you carry him with you in the tabernacle of your heart.

Accept his bequest graciously and willingly. Allow the true and Real Presence of Jesus in this eucharistic gift to open your eyes that you may see his face, open your ears that you may hear his message, open your heart that you may love him unreservedly, turning over without hesitation everything you are.

Let this meeting with Jesus be a time of healing in mind, body, spirit, and heart.

SECTION 1

I
Believe

"I believe; help my unbelief!"

MARK 9:24

I BELIEVE, my eucharistic Jesus. I believe in the Father who created us for no other reason than love. I believe that when we faltered, the Father sent you to pick us up and dust us off, which meant mingling with us and getting right into the fracas. I believe that you came willingly, through the power of the Holy Spirit and the acceptance of our Blessed Mother.

I believe that you spent thirty-three years walking this earth, preparing yourself for your ultimate sacrifice, and three years preparing us for dealing with life after you returned to the Father. I believe that you sent the Holy Spirit, and ever since that first Pentecost, it is the Spirit who guides us and gives us spiritual strength through grace.

I believe that you accepted the most ignominious death one could imagine to make things right for us after we polluted the waters pretty much beyond recognition. I believe that you loved us so intensely and so unconditionally that you came up with an idea that continues to live on our altars and in our hearts to this very day.

I believe that you rose three days after we executed you and that you put death forever in proper perspective. I believe, dear Jesus, that you will come again in glory and that your plan for me is that I spend eternity with the triune community of love we call the Trinity in the peace and joy of your kingdom.

I believe that you are present here in the Eucharist, not just symbolically, but really honest-to-goodness present Lord Jesus, and that the intensity of your love is why you cared enough to do this for us. I believe that you love each and every person equally and that every one of us has a claim on you. I believe, Jesus. From the bottom of my heart, I believe.

Now that I think about it, there's no wonder that I believe in you. You have never given me any reason not to, my Lord. I'll tell you something that truly is remarkable, though. Amazing beyond my most creative imagination is that you, the Savior of the universe, believe in me. Oh my, thank you!

Amen.

Just as you did it to one of the least
of these...you did it to me.

OH, LORD, I am truly happy to be here with you. I love our quiet time together, just the two of us. It's peaceful. It's calm. There's a restfulness I find nowhere else. What a gift, Lord. What a gift!

I love you in the Eucharist. Let me remember, though, that while I am called to love you here, present as the Body of Christ on this altar, I am called also to be present to members of the body of Christ when I leave here.

As I warm myself by the fire of your love, let me not be oblivious to those who, like you, have nowhere to rest their weary heads or shelter their fragile bodies from the biting cold or stifling heat.

As my soul is fed by the bread of angels, let me not only *think* of those who have no food to fill the emptiness in their bodies, but make a concrete plan to actually *do* something about it.

As I drink in the reality of your eternal love for us, let me be aware of those who thirst for peace and justice. Put it on my heart to do everything possible in my own corner of the universe to bring the gift of your peace.

As I experience your love for me in this sacrament I was taught to love, let me be committed to introducing you to those who never met you or who have forgotten who you are. Give me a sense of urgency to share you with people who may otherwise never get to meet you.

Make me conscious that while you invited me to come and be with you here present on this altar, you also called me to be present to my brothers and sisters. You outright told me that whatever I do to the least of them, I do to you.

Teach me to know when you want me to be here with you and when you would prefer that I worship you by serving others or maybe sharing time with friends who need to be with me instead. Never let this become simply routine. Show me how to keep a balance. Help me resolve to spread your Word that I profess to believe. I want to share my time, talent, and treasure without reserve to make that a reality, Lord.

Amen.

"Why does he eat with tax collectors and sinners?"

MARK 2:16

BELOVED JESUS, I adore you and praise you for all that you are and all you call me to be. It is such a blessing to be here.

We live in a world where many people attach a particular significance to being seen with people of renown. A photograph taken with the president or an autograph of a baseball player is worth showing our friends with a certain amount of enthusiasm. If the archbishop walks into a room and calls us by name, people take note. Being seen at dinner with certain individuals might make some people feel important. Sometimes we forget that it certainly gets no more special than this.

Right here I am sharing a priceless Emmanuel moment with you, dear Jesus. You, my Savior, have willingly consented not only to being seen with me, but to sharing an interactive exchange where I speak to you and you speak to my heart. You have not simply autographed a piece of paper with your name, but you have signed yourself forever into my heart. You actually take delight in the time we spend together, calling every single one of us by name and allowing each and every person the confidence of knowing you personally—of calling you friend. What a concept, Jesus!

Let me accept that intimacy, Lord, and give everything I have to this friendship with you. Let me never forget the intensity of your love, Jesus.

Sometimes you are so readily present that I take you for granted, Lord. Quite honestly, you have never given me any reason not to take you for granted; you are always here for me—for us—no matter what!

Please Jesus, pour into my heart a deep delight in knowing you and being seen with you. Let me speak your name with humble awe that I am so blessed to know you. Sharpen my awareness of you, and never let me be ashamed to let the world know that you are my friend.

Amen.

*"The wind blows where it chooses,
and you hear the sound of it, but you do not
know where it comes from or where it goes.
So it is with everyone who is born of the Spirit."*

JOHN 3:8

SPIRIT OF GOD, I come with praise and gratitude in my heart for the incredible graces you bring to my life. You are truly, truly awesome! Quite honestly, I think you get cheated. We begin each of our prayers in the name of the Father and of the Son and of the Holy Spirit, and then so often we take off in the direction of the Father and/or the Son and leave you behind. That's probably because it's hard for us to get a mental picture of you. But really we don't need a picture. You are so obviously with us.

It was through you, precious Spirit, that Jesus joined the human race. And when he finished his mission he sent you, the Holy Spirit, to dwell among us and to be our advocate. Not only did you come, but you came bearing gifts—like wisdom, understanding, knowledge, counsel, piety, fortitude, and fear of the Lord, to name just a few! Jesus promised you would come, and Pentecost pretty much made it clear that once again, he was true to his word.

I can't see you, but I certainly know you've touched my life, Spirit God, just as you touched those early Christians on that first Pentecost.

I know you whisper softly, giving me encouragement and affirmation to go on when life gets tough.

I know you touch my heart; where else would I have gotten this incredible gift of faith that brought me with longing in my heart to this place where Jesus hides in that wafer of bread?

I am so grateful that you blow gently in my life, Spirit wind.

Please liberate me from my fears and help me defend those who are too weak, too ill, too young, too old, too unborn, or too beaten to survive without help.

Just as you overshadowed our Blessed Mother so that Love was conceived within her, you overshadow each of us so that Love is conceived within us, too. Thank you, Breath of God. Thank you.

Amen.

"Father, into your hands I commend my spirit."

LUKE 23:46

LORD OF OUR HEARTS, as I read through Scripture, it's obvious your every action, your every word, was an invitation to follow you to the Father. But during your last few days on earth, your messages grew even more powerful.

On Holy Thursday evening, you held bread and wine in your hands and said those amazing words of consecration: "This is my body"; "This is my blood," and with them instituted the Eucharist so you could be with us all the days and nights until eternity.

The next afternoon, as *you* hung on *our* Cross, just before you surrendered your life on our behalf, you cried out, "Father, into your hands I commend my spirit."

Oh, my. What an example! Not just at the hour of death, but each and every hour of all the days of our lives. "Father, into your hands I commend my spirit!"

Having learned to know the Father through you, there is no other place I could want to be but in the Father's hands.

I am tired and weary, Lord. Things haven't gone well today, and I feel pretty much like this one was a loss. Father, into your hands I commend my spirit.

Now that I think about it, that remark I made that seemed like such a brilliant retort earlier today—that wasn't such a good thing to say, Lord. It was clipped and biting. Father, into your hands I commend my spirit.

I'm on my way to the hospital to visit a good friend who is extremely ill. This may be the last time I get to see her. We've been good friends for a very long time, but this time I really don't have any idea what I'm going to say. Father, into your hands I commend my spirit.

This was a lovely day, Lord. It was so good to be with my family. We don't have enough days like this. But this one was perfect. Everyone was there. The laughter—oh, the laughter was delightful! We enjoyed this one so much. Father, into your hands I commend my spirit.

Heavenly Father, when I take the time for one of these Emmanuel moments, I get a little closer to Jesus, and I know you a little better as a result. It boggles the mind that we would take the perfect world that you created and mess it up beyond all recognition.

And then, in response, you came up with a plan like this one. Not only to save us from ourselves, but to give us the greatest gift anyone could ever imagine. For your Son to live and die and rise again on our behalf and stay around to be our strength in the good times and the bad—this is truly remarkable. Father, into your hands I commend my spirit.

Amen.

"I am with you always, to the end of the age."

MATTHEW 28:20

JESUS, MY LOVE, no matter how many times I recall the events of your last week of public ministry, each time it comes to my heart with renewed amazement.

Holy Thursday is remarkable! You faced the most humiliating death imaginable because of sin—*our* sin—*my* sin. And still you chose, in the face of it all, to call your friends together at a Passover Seder meal so you could institute the Eucharist.

Even though you knew Judas would betray you...

Even though you knew Peter would deny you...

Even though you knew your friends would abandon you...

Even though you knew the adoring throngs would condemn you...

Even though you knew I would turn my back on you—not once or twice, but on a regular basis, over and over again—you went right ahead and allowed your love for us—rather than anger or wrath at our incredibly poor choices—to motivate the decision you made at the Last Supper.

You knew what a knotted mess humankind was in and what it was going to take on your part to untangle us. And still, on the very night you would begin the journey to your death, you left yourself to us for always and ever.

And that's why I can come here, precious Jesus, and spend this time with you. Not simply to think about you. Not only to remember you. Not just to pray to you off in the distance somewhere. I can come here to share this time with you...actually be here with you present on this altar and living in my heart.

I'll never actually be able to comprehend the magnitude of that, Lord. But I ask you to change my heart so what we commemorate at every single Mass will be the motivation behind what I think, what I do, what I say, and how I live. Let me always allow you to hold me in the palm of your hand—you who allow me to hold you in the palm of mine—and then receive you into my very being.

Thank you, Jesus.

Amen.

"As the Father has loved me, so I have loved you."

JOHN 15:9

LORD, JESUS, present in the Eucharist, you said that you love us as much as the Father loves you. That's truly amazing, Lord! Sometimes we forget just how passionate a proclamation that is!

That love remains on our altars to remind us that there is nothing—absolutely nothing—you wouldn't do for us. And we have your presence here in this host as evidence of that passion.

With each opportunity, you chose to empty yourself of everything you had as proof of that all-encompassing love. From the very beginning, you emptied yourself—the God of the Universe—into Blessed Mary, allowing her to be your Mother, and affording us the greatest gift known to the world. That moment when she knelt in humility and uttered her quintessential "Fiat!" was the beginning of your life as one of us, a complete gift of passionate love and total emptying.

Of course, the ultimate emptying was the passion itself. No greater love...no greater love.

Knowing full well how the course of history would go, you chose to announce to your dinner guests on Holy Thursday night that as the Father has loved you, so also you love us. And in case there could be a doubt of just how dynamic that statement was, you proceeded to empty yourself into a piece of bread and a cup of wine, an act of unreserved meekness and humility.

Further, you invited us to repeat the same act over and over in memory of you. It is a constant reminder of love beyond all telling—the promise to remain with us always—until the end of time.

In response, you ask love to be the core of our existence, the motivation of our actions, and the focus of our thoughts.

It sounds like a good idea here, Lord, but sometimes I forget. I allow my own personal agenda to undermine your plan for me. Help me leave here newly committed to love you more today than yesterday and more tomorrow than today. Allow my love for you to grow in intensity and passion.

Jesus, you are Emmanuel: God with us. Keep me aware of your unreserved emptying of yourself. Help me return your love by emptying myself of all selfishness, accepting your love in its place. Let me become every bit as much a receptacle of who you are as that monstrance that rests on the altar before me holding the Bread of Life.

Amen.

"No one has greater love than this..."

JOHN 15:13

SO, JESUS, when you laid down your life for us, you had already performed the greatest act of love in sacrificing yourself totally.

You could return to your Father after the resurrection, having given everything you had to us and for us. But no! You decided to go another step and give us the Eucharist, the sacrament of You-With-Us-Always.

The choice of that kind of vulnerability truly boggles the mind, Lord. In that eucharistic plan is your unspoken willingness to be completely defenseless in what appears to be a simple piece of bread.

You have put yourself literally in our hands, Lord. Someone has to make the bread. Someone has to consecrate it. And once you are present, you are subject to remaining there, waiting. If no one comes, you can't just get up and leave. If someone treats you with disrespect, you have no means of self defense. If we choose to ignore you, you are here for the duration...no matter what! And if we want a relationship with you, you are here always, patiently and lovingly awaiting our arrival. Oh my, what a gift you are, Jesus!

Another complete and total giving on your part, not just a loan for a week or two, but for always! There truly is no greater love than this! Let me never take you or this awesome gift of Eucharist for granted, Lord. Let us always be aware that there is no greater love than you have already shown in your passion and death and that you continue to show in this awesome gift of the Eucharist.

Thank you, dear Jesus, not only for that extraordinary gift, but also for the faith to believe in your Real Presence here.

I adore you, precious Jesus,

...in the simplicity of your humble walk here on earth among us;

...in the glory of your splendor at the right hand of the Father;

...in the miracle of the Eucharist at every single Mass and right here on this altar.

In response, let me give everything of myself back to you without reservation.

Amen.

SECTION 2

I Will
Love

*"You must therefore set no bounds to your love,
just as your heavenly Father sets none to his."*

MATTHEW 5:48 (THE NEW JERUSALEM BIBLE)

PRAISE TO YOU JESUS present here in that host. I love you from a burning deep within my very being. In the calm reverence of this church, how can I help loving you with everything in me, Lord?

But you asked me to love beyond the walls of this building. You asked me to see you and believe in you when the setting isn't so lovely and the circumstances aren't so peaceful.

Please, Lord, give me grace to see you in the face of the obnoxious man at the bus stop who talks loudly early in the morning when we'd like a little quiet time. And besides, he has an unpleasant smell about him. You are within him, Lord. Let me see you there.

Help me see you in the officious secretary who makes it difficult to see her boss. Honestly, Lord, you'd think she owned the place or something. You are within her, Lord. Let me see you there.

Our children need our love most when they are most unlovable. At those times, you are there, Lord. Let me see you.

Let me see you in the people who disagree with me. If they'd just listen, maybe they'd understand their error.

But, they won't listen, Lord. They think we're the ones who don't know the score. How annoying is that! You are within those people, Lord. Let me see you there.

Let me see you in all people, Lord—those I love deeply and those I can barely abide. Let me allow others to see you in me, even when I am less than who you call me to be. Remind me often that you love each and every one of us the same!

As I see you so clearly in that host before me, Jesus, please continually remind me that your presence in this church is meant to give me the strength and the will to see you when I walk out of here. I ask this and all things in your holy name.

Amen.

"I am the bread of life."

JOHN 6:48

ALL-LOVING AND COMPASSIONATE JESUS, I come here to you with a grateful heart to praise and thank you for this incredible gift of the Eucharist. That you would do this for us is awesome, Lord. Truly awesome!

Some people see this as mere symbolism. A piece of bread that *represents* you—a *sign* of what you said and did at the Last Supper—a mere *memory* of something that happened twenty centuries ago. But faith tells me this is way beyond symbolism. You, dear Jesus; body, blood, soul, and divinity; true God and true Man; the second person of the divine community of love we call the Trinity—you are truly here with me in this Emmanuel moment.

From the depths of my heart, I praise you, the God-man who gave everything you had for us and then stayed around to help us respond to your call to follow you. My love for you is a pittance in comparison to your love for me, and yet I give it to you in all humility, offering myself to you in gratitude for who you are and all you do.

I thank you from the innermost corners of my heart that faith tells me you are right here, even though I can't see you in that little piece of bread. I believe in this miracle from the core of my being, beloved Jesus.

Please, Lord, help me to live my life so in sync with you that I not only see you present in the Eucharist, but that I go out and see you in the people who will cross my path. Help me to live in keeping with your will for me. Let me always serve those I encounter as though I were kneeling right here in front of you in that monstrance, loving and praising you in my brothers and sisters as I do right here and now.

Help me to accept the grace to be unyielding in my faith, willing to speak up and stand firm in what I believe—in the face of a world that finds those who believe in you countercultural and out of step. May I never buckle under the pressure of the secular world in circles where you are unaccepted at best and bitterly hated at worst.

Let me see your beauty in others and spread your word with every chance I get, Lord.

Please, Jesus, help me to see you in the Eucharist and in the Eucharist to see all things.

Amen.

"I am the vine; you are the branches."

JOHN 15:5

GOOD AND GENTLE JESUS, thank you for saving us from ourselves. And thank you, Lord, for all the beautiful suggestions you gave us on how to live. Your stories give us so much hope, Lord. In one of your proclamations about our relationship with you, you spoke of yourself as the vine and us as the branches. On first hearing, the message would seem to be that you are our lifeline. You are where we get our strength, our food, our ability to grow and flourish. And, there is something to that.

But a closer examination reveals so very much more. A trip to a vineyard allows us to see that no fruit grows on the vine. It *only* grows on the branches. So as we think deeper, we realize you are saying you have a plan of partnership for us.

As the God of the universe, you could certainly bring forth the fruit of the kingdom without help. And yet, Lord Jesus, in the almost unfathomable passion of your love, your plan is to include us to a point where there is no fruit without our cooperation.

You actually engineered a plan to *need* us. The fruit grows only on the branches that are connected to the lifeline of the vine. Thank you, Jesus, for the incredible trust you had that we would stay connected with you, garnering our strength from you, and thriving in your vineyard, allowing clusters of faith to burst forth in your kingdom.

Thank you for that beautiful partnership where we grow stronger and healthier with you coursing through us with the sap of your Holy Spirit. Thank you for caring so much about us that you allow us to be pruned by the Father when we need it, making it possible for us to grow and flourish.

Thank you for allowing the life of who you are to flow through our very beings, calling us into partnership with you in bringing forth the fruit of your kingdom.

My eucharistic Jesus, it is truly mind-boggling that the intensity of your love for us overshadows any misgivings you might have had that we wouldn't come through for you. Allow me, Lord, to stay connected with you, not only so you can be my own life source, but so that I can be true to the trust you had in me.

This is love beyond all telling. Praise you, Lord, for the honor and privilege of being in partnership with you.

Amen.

"Do this in remembrance of me."

JESUS, PRECIOUS JESUS, we praise you for the gift of the Eucharist, for the reality of your Body and Blood that is with us always until the end of time. We thank you, Jesus, for giving us your very being to nourish us and be our sustenance.

Here in the silence with you, Lord, allow me to plunge myself deeper and deeper into the passion of your love.

Beloved Jesus, I can never express the all-consuming love of God in the Eucharist. At each Mass, the presider follows your example and pours wine into a cup. Then he adds just a few drops of water. He subsequently bends over that cup, and in an act of cooperation between the Church and the Holy Spirit, he speaks your words, Jesus: "This is my blood...." *Everything* in that cup is transformed. The water has mingled with the wine and the wine has become your precious blood poured out for us.

Let me, Lord Jesus, be like the water in the eucharistic cup, allowing the Spirit of God to engulf me and com-penetrate with me so completely—as the water does with the wine—that I will be transformed into a new creation in and through you. Let me become so immersed in you that I diminish until there is nothing left of me, and only you remain!

Amen.

"Follow me."

JESUS, PRINCE OF PEACE, at the beginning of his Gospel, John tells how you looked at the unlikely men before you and spoke to them (and us as well) an awesome invitation. You said, simply, "Follow me." And at the end of his Gospel, John tells how you issued the very same invitation.

"Follow me," you said one final time. In the three years between, you lived a constant example of how you wanted us to go about it. The invitation was a request that we be like you. It wasn't a suggestion that we become religious, but that we be spiritual. Not to say prayers, but to be prayerful. Not to do things, but to become someone.

It was an invitation to be yours, to wear your name, to be a Christian. It is a personal, individual call from God to each one of us, to cooperate with the Holy Spirit, to accept the Spirit's grace and to change from within our relationship with ourselves, with our God, with each other—in fact, with the entire world.

You invited us to spread your peace. Lord, in response, I come here to ask your mercy for all the ways in which I have contributed to a lack of peace. I ask, Lord, that you help me see where I have been hurtful in my personal relationships, unloving in my actions, and cutting in my speech.

Let me see where I have contributed to the hostility in the world, sometimes by what I do, but also by the way I close my eyes and pretend I don't see things that might be uncomfortable for me.

Put on my heart the overwhelming commitment to be a transmitter of peace. Let me be so dedicated to your invitation that I stop short of nothing but living each moment for you, establishing constantly the kingdom of God on earth.

Help me respond to your invitation to follow you with an enthusiastic "Here I am, Lord. I come to do your will."

Amen.

> *"First be reconciled to your brother or sister,*
> *and then come and offer your gift."*

MATTHEW 5:24

LORD, with all my heart I praise you for who you are and all you do for me. I am always amazed at your goodness and patience with me and the generosity of your unconditional love. You are so free with your gifts. Thank you mostly for your gift of peace.

When you left us, you said, "Peace I leave with you. My peace I give to you." You yourself are the peace you left with us, aren't you, Lord? This was just one more way of you telling us you planned to stay here with us! Please help me accept that gift of your peace—yourself—with every fiber of my being. I so much need your peace, Lord. I so much need you!

I pray desperately for peace in my heart. Less resentment. Less anxiety and frustration in situations I can't control. I ask that you lead me ever so gently to allow peace to grow where it isn't. In each aspect of my life where there is an unmended fence, whether it was a minor infraction or a major devastation, help me put peace. Whether it is a faint semi-memory from years ago or a scar from a recent conflagration, please help me put peace. If it means forgiving or asking forgiveness, if it means hanging on or letting go, if it means giving or accepting, please put me at just the right place at just the right time so I can spread peace. When I pray for world peace, remind me that it starts in my heart.

Peace isn't just something, Lord, it's someone. Be the someone I bring with me through my life to leave your peace behind me wherever I go. You promised us your peace. Allow me the privilege of helping to fulfill your promise, Jesus.

Amen.

"No one has greater love than this,
to lay down one's life for one's friends."

JOHN 15:13

LOVING SAVIOR, praise and thanks to you for this quiet time with you. When you say you love me, I have no doubt. You gave everything you had to fix my brokenness. You did it for me!

When you say you love me, I can't question it for a minute as I experience your presence in this host. You do it for me!

When you say you love me, I can't wonder at your motive. You have shown over and over again that you love—without question, without doubt, without reserve—each and every person. You do it for us; you do it for me.

And Jesus, what do you ask in return? That I love you back. Can you tell that I do love you? Or do I leave room for doubt? Can I always say without reservation that what I do, I do for you?

Well, I brought dinner to my neighbor after she had surgery. Did I do it for you? Or did I do it for the warm fuzzy I felt when she thanked me?

I put pretty much money in the collection—a larger percentage than they ask. Do I do it for you? Or do I do it because it makes me feel like a big shot?

Whenever they ask for volunteers, I'm always the first one to say, "I'll do it." Do I do it for you? Or do I do it because I need to keep busy and, when I don't, I have too much time to think and face who I am?

Jesus, you and I both know when I can say I did it for you and when I have some ulterior motive. Please clear my heart of all pride and allow me, Lord of my heart, to serve you free of guile—you who did it all for me! Let me never resent the time or the effort required.

Let me always do what you ask of me, precious Jesus, as you did what the Father asked of you. Let me do it for you.

Lord, please give me purity of motive and cleanliness of heart so that when life is over and I stand before the throne of the Father, I can say in sincere honesty, "I did it for you!"

Amen.

SECTION 3

I Am
Forgiven

"Your sins are forgiven."

LUKE 7:48

MERCIFUL AND COMPASSIONATE JESUS, thank you for loving me into this relationship. The fire of your love burns within me, calling me to an ever growing and closer friendship with you. And yet, the more I come here, the more I realize how little I give in response to your generosity. The more I know, the more I realize how little I know. The more I love, the more I realize how little I love. The closer I am to you, Lord, the more I realize how much forgiveness I need and how much closer to you I want to be.

Merciful Jesus, I present myself to you with a sense of gratitude for who you are. I ask you in deepest humility to forgive the coldness in my heart, the reluctance in my spirit, and the unwillingness in my response to my fellow human beings.

Guide me to face—head on—my sins, flaws, and failings; the sins I commit and the good things I omit; the "big" sins that are obvious and the "little" ones I try to explain away. Let me not be at ease with even the slightest infraction, knowing that it draws me away from you, Lord, and it affects the entire body of Christ.

Be so much the center of my life that I want only to please you and will go the extra distance to free myself of the sin that doesn't allow you into certain areas of my heart. Let passive aggression and resentment have no place in my life, Lord.

Help me, Jesus, not just to keep the Commandments, but to live the Beatitudes. Give me the grace to put the spirit of the law above the letter of the law. I'm well aware that it's entirely possible to keep the letter of the Commandments and still not live the spirit of Christianity.

Jesus, I want to start fresh right now, letting go of the one pattern in my life that does the most harm. If I know what it is, help me willingly surrender it to you and take it to you in the sacrament of reconciliation. If I haven't chosen to recognize it to this point, please let me see it now as we spend this quiet time together. I love you, Jesus. I need your forgiveness, Lord. And the beauty of it is that you want to forgive me even more than I want to be forgiven.

Thank you, Jesus.

Amen.

"You shall be holy, for I am holy."

PETER 1:16

JESUS, could I talk with you a little bit about holiness, please? Quite honestly, I'm a little afraid of the word "holy," Lord. I know I've repeatedly yielded to the temptation to be less than I am by running from holiness. It's one of those words that seem like they are out of my league. I think of the mystics and martyrs. Hair shirts and unpadded kneelers. But, holiness isn't just for those permanently committed to God by solemn vows. It's for all of us, isn't it, Lord?

Is it okay for someone as ordinary as I am to want to be holy? I want it, but I'm afraid of it. Sometimes I want you so badly I hurt, but then I'm actually afraid to get too close. I'm just not sure, Lord. After all, you *are* God!

As I think over the lives of the saints, I'm more aware of the people who did something magnificent with their lives, but on second thought, there were many who just lived simple, unspectacular, holy, lives. Maybe I could get used to the word "holy" if I didn't always think of the huge accomplishments. Maybe saint with a small "s" isn't so bad.

Help me to realize holiness in my ordinary life, Lord, as you call me to a relationship with you, my awesome God. Help me live my life in and for you, allowing the Holy Spirit to direct me in the ordinary world of family, friends, work, and social life. Help me forget my fear of having to do something outstanding so I can be close to you in common, ordinary, everyday things of life.

Help me develop a conscious awareness of God's incredible love for me and accept the grace to live my life in response to that love. Lead me to talk with you, listen to you, share with you, spend time with you, live in you.

I'm not interested in stifling austerity, but in a living and growing, freeing relationship of love with you. Never let my fear that it might be overwhelming keep me from growing in friendship with you. Teach me how to be holy, Lord. Even if I resist.

Amen.

"Take my yoke upon you, and learn from me;
for I am gentle and humble in heart..."

MATTHEW 11:29

HELLO, JESUS. I love you. Thanks for inviting me. I learn so very much from sharing quiet time with you. You speak so intensely to my heart when I listen to you. One of your many amazing lessons in the Eucharist is humility.

It was in humility,

...that you became one of us.

...that you lived in poverty with no place to lay your weary head.

...that you walked with ordinary people and called as your friends those who had no wealth or position.

...that you washed the feet of your Apostles.

It was in humility that you stood before those who mocked you and scourged you and nailed you to a cross, and you remained silent in the face of such abuse.

The night before your death on the cross, you committed yourself to the humility of the Eucharist. Speak, then, to me of humility, Lord.

I'm not adept at saying a gracious "thank you" when someone compliments me. I'm always tempted to slough it off.

On the other hand, I'm not that great at facing my shortcomings either, Lord. When someone cares enough about me to point out a change I need to make, wow, Lord, that's tough!

That's why I need you to help me work on this humility thing, Jesus. Please let me face myself as I truly am. The way you see me—as ugly as that may be—and as beautiful! All of us have been gifted with talents. It's important to face them and use them according to your plan. It's you I honor when I accept goodness in myself without pride. And, of course, there's a flip side to that. I have to face the reality of my limitations. Pride is such a powerful force, Lord.

Either way, it will take some effort. Neither comes easy to me. During the quiet time I am here, Jesus, put on my heart the gifts and talents you see in me and let me be grateful for them. And then, Lord, let me face where I need to accept your grace to improve. Maybe, Lord, point out something—just one thing—I ignore in myself that really needs work. Help me accept that and give it up to you. Please, Lord, let me be at ease with myself and live in humble acceptance of myself as you see me.

Thanks for staying with us in the Eucharist so I can come to you like this and ask for your help. I love you, Jesus.

Amen.

"And whenever you pray, do not be like
the hypocrites; for they love to stand and
pray in the synagogues and at the street corners,
so that they may be seen by others.
Truly I tell you, they have received their reward."

MATTHEW 6:5

ALL-KNOWING AND MERCIFUL JESUS, I've come here to do a little housekeeping. Will you help me out with that, please? Jesus, you were always able to see behind the façade. Pharisees could never fool you with their surface rituals. Your friends couldn't hide their inner feelings from you by saying one thing but thinking something else. And I can't conceal the corners of my soul where cobwebs camouflage the sins the world can't see.

The Gospel shows how you always had the right words to let people see into the depths of their hearts. And you have the right words for me, too, Lord.

Sometimes I convince myself it's okay to have the unkind thoughts if I don't say the actual words. Sometimes I put a smile on my face when there's resentment in my heart, and I think that makes it all right. Sometimes I allow judgmentalism and self-righteousness to pass as acceptable because I know I'm right, so it's tolerable. Oh, Lord, I'm sorry for that!

Just because the rest of the world can't see what's going on in my heart doesn't mean you can't see it. Help me today, Lord, to look into all the quiet little corners of my soul and get rid of the dust, the grime, the grit, and the soot that hide out there.

I don't want the criteria for what I clean out and what I allow to stay within me to be just what people can see. Please, Lord, help me to remember that it isn't what others can see that's important. It's what you and I know. I turn over to you, Lord, my thoughts, my feelings, and my interior being. I give you my mind and my heart. Remain there so you can help me be true to your plan for me, even in places where it doesn't show in polite company.

Remind me of the secret sins I commit in my heart. Keep me aware of the quiet attitudes that rob me of my interior peace. Lord, let's—you and me—do a little housekeeping in my heart right now

Thank you, Jesus.

Amen.

*"Come to me, all you that are weary
and are carrying heavy burdens,
and I will give you rest."*

MATTHEW 11:28

HELLO, LORD. Thank you for being here. It means the world and all that you are always here and I can come any time.

Okay, Lord. I admit it. I came here to get some sympathy. I can't seem to find it anywhere else so I thought you'd at least listen. Life is tough right now, and no one seems to care. I feel like I'm carrying a big load, and the climb is all uphill.

It gets a little wearisome spending life making a real effort and coming up against unresponsiveness at every turn. I work really hard and continually come up empty-handed. Honestly, Lord, when I speak, I feel like the words are falling on deaf ears. No one pays attention. No one listens.

I'm sick and tired of seeing my hopes and dreams dashed by people who just don't care. I get the car washed, and some inconsiderate truck driver plows through the puddles with no mud flaps and sprays yuck all over my car. I stay late at work trying to catch up and come home to find a litter trail from where the kids came in the door all the way to the television. There are dishes in the kitchen sink and towels on the bathroom floor.

You can't even imagine, Lord, how I feel when I give it my all and no one cares. Oops! Are you laughing yet, Lord? I just realized—truly realized—who I'm talking to here. You know more than anyone what that's like, Jesus. I'm sitting here putting my foot in my mouth, ala Peter. I always picture you laughing at that man and some of his extraordinary gaffes. And, now, I think you're laughing at me. Well, no, you're laughing with me, Lord, because you've allowed me to hear my own words and find them pathetically amusing.

Thanks for putting it in proper perspective for me. Your whole public ministry consisted of you giving it your all and the people around you missing the point, ignoring your message, and ultimately letting you die the death of what appeared, by all human accounts, a failure. And, even though you knew that's the direction it was going, you stayed patiently on course.

Thanks for letting me see that, Lord. You've given me hope. If I walk with you and talk with you on the way, it will be...well, maybe not easy, but certainly worth giving it everything I've got.

Thanks for helping me take myself a little less seriously, Lord.

Amen.

*O Lord, my strength and my stronghold,
my refuge on the day of trouble...*

JEREMIAH 16:19

HELLO, JESUS. You are so incredibly good, Lord, that I feel a little out of line saying this, but I've just got to talk with someone! I'm kind of tired and weary of life right now.

You know, I feel like I'm in one of those hotel lobby revolving doors, trying to get somewhere and winding up where I began with nothing much to show for it!

To tell the truth, I get a little tired of trying so hard and seeing no results. I try to teach the children what's right, but honestly I feel like it's falling on deaf ears. Are they paying any attention at all, Jesus?

There's such a difference between the way men and women think, Lord. I'm never really sure if my spouse and I are on the same track or if we're just passing through life at the same time. There's love there; but I feel like we're missing something.

And my job, Lord? I just keep plugging along, doing the work of people who don't bother to do their share. No one appreciates me, Lord. You have no idea!

Now that I think about it, this is pretty pathetic, isn't it, Lord? I'm sharing my disappointment with the God of the universe and Lord of my heart who put everything he had on the line, only to come up short by human standards!

You healed their children and fed the throngs, and they decided to turn on you. You showed love and compassion, and they yelled "Crucify him." You mended their shattered hearts, and they broke yours. You filled their depleted souls and renewed their spirits, and they drained you dry. Thanks for reminding me and putting that all in perspective, Lord. You do have a very definite idea how unappreciated I feel.

Give me the grace to be patient, Lord, and to remember that there is nothing that burdens me that you didn't carry—and much more—up the hill to Calvary, because you love me. Let me accept my burdens, because I love you back. I think they won't seem so heavy then. Good idea. Thank you, Jesus.

Amen.

*"I will put enmity between you and the woman,
and between your offspring and hers;..."*

GENESIS 3:15

HEAVENLY FATHER—Oh, good and gracious God! As we read the message of Genesis, it is truly a wonder that you would stare our pride in the face and promise us humility in the flesh of your Son; look at selfishness and promise us altruism; catch us red-handed in our sinfulness and promise us redemption. Not a quick fix, but your only Son. Right there on the spot, without hesitation, you promised us Jesus.

Oh my, how very lovely, Father God. With that mentality of the first book of the Hebrew Scriptures, I come to you now.

When we speak of your will but want to follow our own personal wants, give us Jesus.

When we hear the cries of the poor but are tempted to turn a deaf ear, give us Jesus.

When we are presented with a choice and we know what's right, but we prefer what's easy, give us Jesus.

When we have the opportunity to speak up for good but it will be difficult and maybe even embarrassing to let people know where we stand, please, please give us Jesus.

When we call ourselves sacramental people but are tugged in a direction to turn away and reject the grace of the Spirit, give us Jesus.

Each time we look into the eyes of a fellow human being...

Each time we come here to pray before the white wafer in the center of the monstrance...

Every time we unite ourselves in Communion with the Holy Sacrifice of the Mass...

Each and every time we approach the altar to receive the Bread of Angels...

Every time we have a chance to bring peace where it isn't, let us be keenly aware, Father, that once a long, long time ago in an incredibly lush and fertile garden, you stared our unspeakable sin square in the eye, and out of pure love for us, made the decision to give us Jesus.

Amen.

"Who am I that I should go to Pharaoh,
and bring the Israelites out of Egypt?"

EXODUS 3:11

JESUS, DEAR, I'm a little insecure these days. Overwhelmed even. I don't know, Lord, I feel ill-prepared to do your will for me. When I pray, I, like so many of those who have gone before me, have a whole list of "Yes, buts..." in response to what you suggest.

I just don't think I can do what you ask. It's too hard. I never think I'm capable. That might sound like humility, but it isn't. It's fear, I guess, more than anything. And pride, too. I'm afraid to fail. Afraid I'll look ridiculous. But I know in my heart that when you call me to do something, Jesus, you plan to be right there with me. All I have to do is be open to your Holy Spirit.

What happened to Moses can happen to each of us, can't it, Lord? Even me. He wasn't much of a guy, really. A murderer, a coward! Duplicitous. A fugitive. No one would have held tremendously high hopes for Moses. Least of all, Moses himself. He was ordinary. It was God who was extraordinary. It's when ordinary people meet up with our extraordinary God that it's time to take off our shoes, because the ground on which we stand is, indeed, very, very holy! Moses could do it all, once he stood beside the all-consuming fire of God's love in that bush.

In the face of your all-consuming love for me in that host, Lord, I too can do literally anything. I'm not an extraordinary person who makes a monumental difference in the world. I am a very ordinary person who makes decisions, makes dinner, makes love, makes waves, makes plans, and makes mistakes.

I also make a promise to you in the light of your promise to me. You said you'd stay here until the end of time. And here you are, living up to that in the most amazing way.

What do I promise in return? I promise to give myself to you. I promise, a little reluctantly I admit, to put my fear and pride in your hands. I promise to trust in your plan for me.

Then, no matter what it is, I can do it, Lord. I can rest in the peace of knowing you trust in me. Thank you for that, Lord. Please help me to let you live in and work through me. It's your will and not my wants that count here. Let's face the near and distant future together.

Amen.

SECTION 4

I Will
Follow

Do not fear, for I have redeemed you;
I have called you by name, you are mine.

ISAIAH 43:1.

HELLO, LORD. I'm back. Are you surprised? I'm not surprised that you're here. You are always here! I'm not *surprised*. But I am *amazed*! Never let me lose that sense of wonder at you being here always and ever! As a kid, I always liked places like this where I could go that seemed safe and secluded—a tree house—a little cave in the rock hill—the side of a huge tree that couldn't be seen from the road. It always gave me a sense of security—that place I knew about—and usually a few others knew about it also. We thought we were special because we had those places that were "ours." We felt like we belonged when we went to those places.

We are big into identity, Lord. We like belonging, being in the group. We pledge allegiance to the flag; as children we make the Boy or Girl Scout Promise; we have great pride in being inducted into our sorority or fraternity and knowing the secret sign.

We like being asked to join the club or invited to a place one has to "belong" in order to get in. No one likes to be left out. If there's one thing that makes me feel awful, Lord, it's being on the outside with my nose pressed against the window, watching everyone who belongs having a good time inside. Belonging is very important to all of us, Lord.

We are American. We are Christian. We are Catholic.

But most importantly, we are yours. Let that be the "belonging" that motivates how I look at all the rest of my "belongings."

You have called me, and I am yours. The very thought that you call me by name sends chills right up my spine, Lord. I don't need to "belong" to a club; I belong to you, and nothing else matters. Please help me remember that when I'm fretting about whether I'll get to be part of the "in" crowd. It really doesn't matter, does it? But sometimes it seems like it does. Please don't let that hurt so badly, Lord. Just let me be happy that I belong to you.

Amen.

"Not everyone who says to me, 'Lord, Lord,' will enter the kingdom of heaven, but only one who does the will of my Father in heaven."

MATTHEW 7:21

I ADORE YOU, PRECIOUS JESUS. I believe that you are present here—true God and true man. Allow me to give myself to you totally, Lord. I come to you just as I am. This is not about me, Lord. It is about you. You are what matters, and you desire that I come to you—in whatever condition—to become one with you. Sometimes I'm a little too preoccupied with myself to focus on you.

Help me forget me and abide in you. Take my mind that I may know you better. Take my will that I may serve you with resignation. Take my body and my senses that each may glorify you as I use it for your purposes, to the fullest extent of my ability. And especially, Jesus, take my heart that I may love you deeply and passionately without reserve. Let me give everything of *myself* to you in this sacrament of *yourself.*

Let me forget my own personal agenda and allow you to be my only agenda. Let me set aside my plans to be totally in sync with your incredible plan. Let me give up my wants in favor of your will. Let there be less of me and more of you, Dear Jesus. I offer you my free will that my choices may be your choices, precious Lord.

Grant that my joy comes only in attuning myself to that instant in time when you spoke the words of consecration for the first time, that moment when unconditional love decided to stay with us forever.

Let those words: "Take and eat..." "This is my body..." "Drink you all of this..." "This is my blood..." echo through my very being, becoming the driving force by which I live my every day. Take the first place in my life, allowing nothing to cloud my vision of who you are. Send your Holy Spirit to free me of all that isn't you.

Amen.

At the name of Jesus every knee should bend, in heaven and on earth and under the earth,...

PHILIPPIANS 2:10

JESUS, at the mere mention of your beautiful name—*Jesus*—every knee should bend in heaven, on the earth, and under the earth! Let my heart bend, too, Lord. Let it bend with flexibility to what the Father wills of me. Let it bend to the whisperings of the Holy Spirit.

Let it bend patiently when I have plans of my own and someone asks a favor, or when I see a person in need of my time and I'd rather not give it.

Let it bend in acceptance when I pour all my energy into a project, envisioning a successful outcome, and it turns out to be a disappointing flop.

Let it bend when I don't get what I want, but my friend who didn't even care got it instead.

Let it bend in humility when I feel like a misfit!

Let it bend when things are pretty much going my way and I'm tempted to be just a little smug as I ride the crest of the wave.

Let it bend in submission when I ask you in prayer to do something my way and you choose to do it your way, because you know what's best for me.

Yes, Jesus, let my heart bend with love for you because you are the God who cared enough to save me from my self-chosen disasters. Every time I walk into a church and my knee bends out of reverence, let my heart bend out of love and gratitude. Let me always remember that you are so totally awesome, Jesus, that my whole being—all that I am—has every reason to bend before you, not only here in the Eucharist, but in every person I encounter.

Amen.

"Let it be with me according to your word."

LUKE 1:38

DEAR JESUS, please open my heart to adore you as your Blessed Mother, Queen of the Cenacle, did in her intimate mother-son relationship with you. From the beginning, she believed in you with every breath she took.

Her Immaculate Heart, on fire with love, was the first to adore you in Nazareth within her virginal womb.

At Bethlehem, her maternal love was your first birthday present—the original act of faith.

At Cana, she was the first to recognize your power and offer your gift of service to humankind from her heart of love.

On Calvary, she stood silently worshipping at the foot of your altar-of-a-cross, uniting herself with your passion.

Upon your ascension and return to the Father, we can only imagine her intimate maternal relationship with you in the Eucharist. I can't even imagine the joy in her heart when she received your precious body and blood and held you once again within her, recreating that humbling mother-son bond.

What an awesome Emmanuel (God with us) moment it must have been every time she came into your presence in the Blessed Sacrament. How she must have treasured that time to be with you and share the innermost thoughts of her heart, to relinquish her entire being into your loving presence, and just be.

Allow me, Lord Jesus, to experience with a loving heart your divine presence as our Blessed Mother did. Help me utter a willing *"Fiat"* to whatever you say to my heart. Let me leave here resolved to adore you in the Eucharist through all the Bethlehems, Nazareths, Calvaries, and Cenacles of my life.

Let me listen attentively as you speak to my heart, and please send your Holy Spirit to help me always to do whatever you tell me to do.

Amen.

Create in me a clean heart, O God...

PSALM 51:10

PRECIOUS JESUS, thank you for you! We are overwhelmed by your love. The magnitude of what you did and continue to do for us is amazing! You are just so good!

We praise and thank you for planting the seeds in our hearts that have grown into a relationship with you in this sacrament. As we are magnetized to your presence on the altar, we ask you to come into our hearts and make them more like you. As we realize how willing you were to give yourself to us in the depths of our sinfulness, Lord, we ask you to pour out the grace we need to follow your example.

And so, Jesus, we pray now for the person who has hurt each one of us most of all and for the person we have most hurt. Allow your forgiveness to be all that remains of those unpleasant circumstances when we forgot who you are and who we profess to be. Give us the grace to forgive and be forgiven with none of the trappings of self-righteousness and complacency.

We pray for those who disagree with us—who vote for people we regard as unfit, who stand for policies we consider obviously undesirable. We ask you to bless those whose opinions differ from ours and those who get on our nerves as they blatantly speak their minds to that effect.

Help us to be tolerant of those whose religious foundation we share but whose approach to it differs from ours. Allow us to be aware that sometimes gray is more desirable than black *or* white. Give us humility when we are right and don't allow us ever to gloat, Lord. You know how often we are wrong, and you overlook it time and time and time again for no other reason than love.

Help us remember to be aware of your choice to dwell within the person we dislike or disdain every bit as willingly as you dwell within us. Allow us, Jesus, to live out our prayer when we come before you and say, "I love you, Lord" by loving—truly loving—each and every one of the Father's children. Help us remember what it means when we choose to call ourselves Christians.

As we present ourselves right here before you, allow us to let you change our prejudices, our preconceptions, our narrow-mindedness, our biases, and our bigotry. Please, Lord, open our hearts, warm our coldness, increase our love, and please, Lord Jesus, make us more like you in our hearts.

Amen.

*For God is not unjust; he will not overlook
your work and the love that you showed for his
sake in serving the saints, as you still do.*

HEBREWS 6:10

DEAR AND PRECIOUS JESUS, praise and glory to you for all you are and all you call me to be. In thanksgiving for allowing this incredible relationship with you, I come on behalf of those who are not blessed in the plethora of ways I am.

Lord Jesus, I offer your goodness for those whose lives are a relentless negative escapade and who never experience the beauty of what is good in their lives.

Lord Jesus, I offer your love for those who know only rejection, abuse, and suffering, and whose ears never hear the words "I love you!"

Lord Jesus, I offer your compassion and forgiveness for those whose lives have been racked by poor choices and who live in a constant state of despair, never realizing that hope is within their reach.

Lord Jesus, I offer your peace for those whose lives are ravaged by war, violence, and discord and who don't know the inner rest that comes with harmony and tranquility of body and spirit.

Lord Jesus, I offer your healing for those who suffer

from critical spiritual, physical, mental, or psychological illnesses and who have no idea where to go to be mended.

Lord Jesus, I offer the Eucharist, Bread of Angels, for those who hunger and thirst, not only for physical sustenance, but for spiritual fullness that can only come from knowing you and experiencing your love.

Lord Jesus, I pray that your presence in our world will fill the voids in these lives. Please Jesus, let me never forget that I am called to be your hands and feet, your heart, and your words, knowing that in serving your people, I serve you.

Amen.

SECTION 5

I Am

Grateful

*"But whenever you pray, go into your room
and shut the door and pray to your Father
who is in secret; and your Father who sees
in secret will reward you."*

MATTHEW 6:6

HELLO, LORD. It's me again! It never ceases to amaze me
that you're here waiting for me to come. Walking in here
is always a breath-taking adventure! Gosh, I love coming
here! I especially love the silence. When I sit calmly in the
quiet glow of that little candle that assures your presence
here, you always share something with my heart, Lord. I
so love when you do that, Jesus. It's just so very hard to
quiet myself down enough for that to happen.

Sometimes my life shouts so loudly around me that I
can't hear myself think. I am pulled in so many directions,
I frequently can't decide which way to go. I've even been
known to speak the unspeakable: "I was so busy today, I
didn't have time to pray!" You and I both know that makes
absolutely no sense whatsoever. If it weren't so pitiful, it'd
be funny!

Just when I think life is getting "back to normal,"
(although I'm not even sure any more what "normal" is),
something comes along to add to the chaos. The pace of
life is so fast, and the noise it makes is sometimes so dis-

sonant. It's very hard for me to settle down and just be. But you can make that happen when I'm here with you, Lord.

Take this time to help me let go of all that is frenzied in the whirlwind of today. Shut down my ears to what's going on outside; allow my lips to speak nothing; permit my entire being to be open only to you and the will of your Father. Allow me, Jesus, just to be, to bask in the serenity that I find here with you. Let there be no distractions that carry me away from you. Clear my mind of all thoughts, even the good ones. With each breath I take, fill my being deeper and deeper with your Spirit until there is room for nothing else. At this Emmanuel moment, be all that matters, Jesus. All that matters.

And when I'm empty of all that is not quiet, speak to me, Lord, for I am listening. Let's enjoy the quiet together.

Amen.

This is the cup of my blood....
It will be shed for you and for all....

EUCHARISTIC PRAYER

GLORY AND PRAISE be to you, gentle and loving Jesus, for your presence with us in the Eucharist. It is beyond our human ability to comprehend that you would choose to sentence yourself to the prison of a piece of bread simply because your love is limitless and you want to be available to us. And yet we believe you are here with us always, because we hold in our hearts the words you spoke at the Last Supper.

Those words voice your plan to remain with us here in the Eucharist. They also make it clear that this is both a general bequest and a specific one.

"This is my body which will be given up for you." That "you" is all-inclusive, Lord. You sacrificed your body for my family, my friends, the rich and the poor, people I love, and those I don't care for, the masses of people in general, and each individual in particular.

Lest there be a doubt, you repeated the process with a cup of wine and you said: "This is the cup of my blood.... It will be shed for you and for all...."

That you would give yourself so completely for all God's children is truly remarkable, Jesus. That you would do it for me personally is amazing! Even if I were the only one, you would make the same choice.

Let me always keep the perspective of both the general and the personal aspects of your incredible gift, Lord. Give me the humility to accept that you would make the same choice, even if I were the only one. Keep me aware also that I don't have a personal hold on you. You came for all humankind.

Never allow me to show false humility by failing to accept that you did everything for me, in effect turning a deaf ear to your promises. Likewise, Jesus, never let me fail to remember that each and every person is the object of your love and your gift of yourself.

During the time we spend together, Lord, enter into the deepest recesses of my heart. Allow me to experience you deeply and really in ways I never have before. But let this not be just a moment of personal ecstasy for me. Let me remember the entire body of Christ, committing myself to share my love for you. Let me live my life aware that you are *mine* and let me touch the life of all the people I encounter knowing you are *theirs*.

Amen.

"And now, you will conceive in your womb
and bear a son, and you will name him Jesus."

LUKE 1:31

Jesus,

What a lovely name you have. To your Mother, it meant
the world and all—that which guided her every action—her
every decision. You were her life.

Jesus,

To Joseph, it meant bringing forth the best—the protec-
tor, the teacher, the talents that lie within us that blossom
when you come into our lives.

Jesus,

To Mary Magdalene it meant intimacy. Not as the sensa-
tionalists of the twenty-first century would suggest, but
a closeness where two hearts love so deeply in spiritual
friendship that they can speak without words.

Jesus,

To the woman at the well, as she progressed in her faith,
it came to mean *Messiah* when you allowed her, a Samari-
tan woman, to be the first missionary in building your
kingdom on earth.

Jesus,

To Peter, like the rest of us, it meant acceptance of who he was, with all the little and big flaws—the impetuous reactions, the thoughtless responses, the disastrous denials. It meant trust. After all the mistakes, your trust in him was the foundation for building your Church.

Jesus,

To the good thief, it meant stealing heaven and the blessings of eternity in response to nothing more than a dying plea to remember him when you entered your kingdom.

Jesus,

It means God who saves. It means forgiveness, compassion, and mercy. It means love beyond all telling. It means trust and hope. It means setting no bounds to your love, so much so that you are willing to lay down your life for your friends.

Jesus,

It means you cared enough about us to leave us the Eucharist—that incredible gift of "you-with-us-until-the-end-of-time"—the reason I can come here to share this time with you.

Jesus,

It is the most beautiful name ever.
No wonder they named you *Jesus.*
It fits you so well!

"Speak, for your servant is listening."

1 SAMUEL 3:10

HERE I AM, LORD. I come to do your will! I'm so grateful to you for staying around to be with us, Jesus. This is truly awesome! I love you and cherish my time here to be with you. You always send me away with peace. I'm not sure why I sometimes put it off, because every single time I come, I'm so pleased that I did.

I'm in a giving mood today, Lord. You said you wanted me to give with a generous heart. So, I'm here to ask your opinion. Do you have a great idea for me? What do you want me to give, Lord? I'm listening. Speak to my heart.

Forgiveness to the person who hurt me deeply?

Kindness to my neighbor who complains constantly?

A gentle word to the woman at church who causes so much trouble?

Let the driver who tailgated me for a mile and a half get in front of me when the lane narrows?

Pray for the politician who stands for everything I (and I'm sure you) can't abide? Doesn't it send ice through you when that person gets on television and fights adamantly for what you and I both know isn't right, Lord? Or is there a middle ground you see that I'm missing? And even if I do have it right, maybe I shouldn't be quite so haughty about it.

Come on, Lord! That's not what I meant at all. I was hoping for something a little more tangible. I was thinking more along the lines of giving to the Heart Fund. And here you are suggesting that I give to *your* Heart Fund. I should have known you'd want me to stretch a bit.

I'll sit here quietly for a while, Lord, and let these thoughts settle into my heart. I know you didn't always feel like doing what your Father asked. Certainly not that really big request. And you did it all. You are truly incredible, precious Jesus.

When I leave here, I'm going to look for the first chance to do something I know you would do, even if I don't feel like it. I'm tempted to ask you to go easy on me, Lord, but instead I ask that you come along to help me do it. Thank you, Jesus.

Amen.

Blessed be the Lord for ever. Amen and Amen.

PSALM 89:52

AMEN, LORD! Yes, I know. Amen is usually at the end of our prayers. This time I'm starting out with it so I pay particular attention to it. Often we rattle off a prayer or two and slide an "Amen" in at the end as though it were nothing more than the period at the end of a sentence.

This time I want to stop and think about it! Amen. *So be it*! It's not simply a punctuation mark. It's a declaration. It's an affirmation. It's an admission of reality. This time, I'm saying it from the heart, Lord.

Jesus, you became one of us so you could fix our brokenness. Amen.

Jesus, you are present here on this altar and on all the altars in the world because you love us unconditionally. Amen.

Jesus, you promised to send the Holy Spirit to guide us and give us strength, and you did exactly that. Amen.

Jesus, you want us to treat each other with respect, to be loving and forgiving, even as your Father is loving and forgiving of us. Amen.

Jesus, you are the Prince of Peace who calls us to be peacemakers in our own hearts, in our families, in our communities, and in our world. Amen.

Jesus, you never said it would be easy if we followed you, but you did promise it would be well worth the effort. Amen.

Jesus, you said you would be with us until the end of time, and you are right here, ready to come with me out to face the world when I leave.

Amen.

Jesus, I believe in who you are, what you promised, and how very much you love me.

Amen.

Jesus, I love you too.

Amen.

Prayer of Thanksgiving
After Eucharistic Adoration

THANK YOU, LORD, for meeting me in the silence. What a gift this is. What a gift *you* are!

Thank you, Jesus, for staying with us even though your mission was complete. Thank you for our time together. It truly gets no better than this, Jesus.

This is a place to go when there's no place to go. When I don't know where to turn, I can turn to you, knowing you will be here. When I don't know what to do, I can listen, knowing you'll speak to my heart. When I can't find an answer, you have one all ready for the asking. When no one else cares, you do. When I'm so happy I could burst, you'll share the joy with me. When I fall, you'll pick me up. If I need forgiveness, you're just the person to take care of that. There is nothing—absolutely nothing—I can't bring in here to share with you. It doesn't make any difference what's going on in my life, Lord. You are here in the silence! And, I am welcome any time, 60/60/24/7/365.

You being God and everything, this could be an austere experience. After all, this is a private audience with the God of the universe and the Savior of my soul. But you make it so unthreatening. I'm never intimidated when I come here. That's because your words two thousand years ago were just the right ones to create calm in my heart today. How incredibly awesome is that!

I've enjoyed this time with you, Lord. Let's do it again real soon. I love you, Jesus.

Amen.

Other Titles on the Eucharist from Liguori Publications

Treasures Holy and Mystical
A Devotional Journey for Today's Catholics

Fr. Powell once again reminds us of the power and popularity in uncovering treasures of the Church for our modern lives. The litanies, novenas, and rosary prayers are reminiscent of their traditional Catholic origins and speak to the hearts of today. Included are seven new novenas for the modern world, three mystical novenas, and ten new litanies focused on a journey toward holiness and "partakers" in God's divine being (2 Peter 1:4).

ISBN 978-0-7648-1913-1

The Eucharist
From Liguori's **50 Questions From the Pews** *series*

Designed to bring a better understanding of the Eucharist and the rituals involved in Mass, devotion, and prayer, this book is formatted in a way that is easy to read and understand. As it shows how prayer and worship form the core of the spiritual renewal of the Catholic community, this book addresses these questions and more: Is there a relationship between the altar and the Eucharist? What is the difference between the Sacred Heart of Jesus and the Eucharistic Heart of Jesus? What is Benediction? Religious and devotional practices are the language we use to communicate with God. *50 Questions From the Pews: The Eucharist* helps the reader participate more fully and richly in the Eucharist.

ISBN 978-0-7648-1699-4

Condensed version also available (Spanish only)
20 Preguntas del Pueblo: *La Eucaristía*
ISBN 978-0-7648-1761-8

For prices and ordering information,
call us toll free at 800-325-9521
or visit our Web site, www.liguori.org.

CPSIA information can be obtained
at www.ICGtesting.com
Printed in the USA
JSHW071053210123
36392JS00003B/11